REINCARNATION WITHIN CHRISTIANITY

REINCARNATION
within
CHRISTIANITY

Evelyn Francis Capel

TEMPLE
LODGE
PRESS

First edition 1980
Reprinted 1988

Cover design by Paulo Frank Boer

British Library Cataloguing in Publication Data

Capel, Evelyn Francis
Reincarnation within Christianity.
1. Christianity and reincarnation
I. Title
129   BR115.R4

ISBN 0-904693-08-2

Made and printed in Great Britain by
Temple Lodge Press
London

Contents

Reincarnation Within Christianity

Reincarnation? Shall I live on earth again? Have I been here
before? Who, me? Who, you? What about the others? What is it
all about? Reincarnation is a real question for all and everyone.
If it applies to me, it applies likewise to others. It is an awkward
kind of question because it has no ifs and buts. It is not strictly
speaking about belief, but about fact. Human souls live more
than once on earth or they do not. Some people believe one thing
and some another and yet in reality they stand before the same
question, dismayed by the experience that belief or unbelief will
not alter the facts.

At the present time the thought of reincarnation has become
thinkable for many in the Western world for whom it is a new experience. Down the ages of history it has been accepted as a
matter of fact in the Eastern part of the world. It sank for centuries into the unknown in the West and emerges again as a question. It is no longer to be ignored, but it can only be encountered
by taking into consideration many factors in human life on which
the mind will feel the need to reflect.

Memory

It can be puzzling, when approaching the idea of reincarnation,
to realise that very few people recall the experience of another
lifetime. That which is termed "far memory" is a rarity. It may
happen that one or the other tells stories about a lifetime long ago
in the same manner that he would speak of his childhood. Others,
with the help of dreams, hypnosis and other inducements, can produce pictures which sometimes correspond to that which can be
discovered by research into history. Such pictures in the memory,
in spite of their charm, are not in fact evidence of other lives or
other events. How is it ever possible to know that the dreamer who
dreams of a mediaeval character has in fact seen an earlier version
of himself? Dreams are at the best hard to evaluate correctly in

waking life. Convincing as they may be to the dreamer, it would be too much to expect that other people could take them at their face value. One is obliged to reflect on a wider issue, the nature of human memory itself. All thoughts about reincarnation tend to produce just this effect that a wider consideration has to be given to the nature of human life and human history.

Remembering and forgetting are functions of the human soul. A person is not only the sum of his conscious impressions and recollections. It is a well known fact that what is forgotten sinks down into the constitution, affects the health and habits. Use is made of the process whenever any kind of skill is to be acquired. Skill will be found to be the result of efforts to learn consciously, which are transformed through practice into unconscious movements and habits, into efforts which have been changed by being forgotten. This process can be completed in one lifetime according to observation. The fact opens up another line of thought about memory if it is considered that the same process can be carried out over a much longer stretch of time, from one life on earth to the next. Each one of us is bigger than the sphere of his self-consciousness, bigger than the sum of his present memories, than the sum of his participation in present history. To find a real picture of reincarnation means reflection upon the effects of forgotten memories on a person's character. If observations are made of his unconscious habits, the way he walks, habitual gestures and the fashion of his constitution, in this deeper layer of memory more will be found to indicate the past than anything he himself can recollect. What such a person once was is then experienced outside the uncertain range of his dreams, memories and personal predilections. The objective language spoken by the built in, forgotten memories, will tell more than pictures in dreams.

The reality of reincarnation can only be studied in terms of such research as that done by Rudolf Steiner and other workers in Mysticism into the profound changes which human beings undergo from one part of a lifetime to another, from the changing conditions of sleeping and waking. How much greater are the changes to be expected from one lifetime to another, from the change produced in death and the process of being born again.

Death and Birth

Reflecting upon death leads to the consideration of what the soul has to part with in the process of leaving the body. That which is temporal and passes away is all that which builds up the personality that has been produced by the forces of heredity and environment, by nationality and sex. Certain influences from these factors will be absorbed by the soul and taken far into the life after death. But the conditions which they have produced disappear with the body. The human spirit is liberated from their limiting power. A poet of the first World War, Wilfred Owen, wrote of a dream which he had in the trenches. He met another soldier from whom he felt a warm friendship and understanding and as he woke, he realised that this was one of his enemies, killed in a battle against him the day before. The battle had made friends of two enemies. What had been personal and one-sided before was transformed by the magic touch of death the next. In dying the personality which is to the fore here on earth ceases to trouble the soul which has entered the Universe.

Nevertheless, the personal experiences are not without significance. When the old personality is cast off, the effects of past experiences are carried by the departing spirit into the realms where they can be changed into something for the future. A process that could be described as a great cosmic one of digestion takes place beyond the Gate of Death. The eternal soul will emerge from the world in which his companions have been people, animals and plants known in the settings of landscapes and interiors into surroundings in which the Hosts of Heaven receive him. He will become a citizen of the Universe, learning what it means to be human in the presence of Angels, Archangels, and all the Company of Heaven. Reincarnation is an idea of such magnitude that, reflecting upon it, one has likewise to consider that which can be called the nature of God.

Death and birth are the biggest events of change that can ever happen. Before a soul can be born there must be a long period of existence within the Universe of God. St. Paul pointed out in his writings that here on earth we live in a world which is like a reflection in a mirror, but before birth and after death the soul stands face to face with divine realities. A soul passing through the Gate of Birth into life in the body emerges from the potent living world

of God into the region of the mirror on earth. Here he begins to
discover what it is to have a will of one's own and to see the
reflection of oneself in what one has done. ''I made it myself'',
proclaims the child who has made this discovery. In the existence
before birth, in the regions of the Universe, there is no space for
human will. The beings of wisdom and strength, who work the will
of God, are too powerful for human souls, who live in the stream
of their influence and activity. Self-consciousness and self-will
do not develop amid such conditions. The human being on his own,
developing self responsibility, is to be found on earth. He is
sheltered there from overwhelming cosmic influences because he
sees in the mirror and not face to face as he did before birth.
Under such conditions his humanity can develop and he can begin
to find himself. In the life before birth he has found God with
all his manifold powers. After birth he will be able to find himself and look in prayer towards the Being of God out of whom he has
been born.

It is an experience of great value for the incarnated soul,
standing with his feet on the earth and his head lifted up to the
Heavens, to feel himself as an individual soul reaching out to
God as the One Heart and Soul of the Universe. The inner attitude
which says to God, ''there are you, here am I'' has been learnt by
human souls in the course of history, especially through the
event of the Protestant Reformation. But in the life before birth
and after death and at intervals in between, the human soul en-
counters the ordered world of beings in their ranks that are known
in theology as the Heavenly Hierarchies. They are as much part
of the Godhead as the powers of my mind and the energies of
my limbs are part of the person whom I call me. To know something of the spiritual nature of the Universe is to have learnt
about the nine ranks of Angels, Archangels and all the Company
of Heaven, who work out of the will of God.

The one-ness of God and the manifoldness of God are as real
as the one-ness and variety within my own human nature. In the
world of the mirror they are known by their influences and effects.
In the world beyond the Gates of Death and Birth, they are encountered face to face in all their glory. The human soul that
passes through their world is influenced and moulded by their
wisdom. They it is who made him human at the beginning. They
re-make him when he comes out of a life on earth into their healing

4

presence. Within their living wisdom, the experiences of a lifetime are digested and re-vitalised by the powers of divine justice. It is no matter of thought but of the creative will to re-make through which the consequences of the past produce the person of time to come. That which the human soul offers out of his past life to the wise and mighty beings of God, becomes his own again for the future in new shape. The soul will accept in the time to come what he has made of himself, but he will not have made it alone, but through the helping wisdom of the gods who are working his transformation.

When the soul comes again to the Gate of Birth he will be sent out into the earth by the divine beings who have fostered him during his time in the Universe. He will have been on a journey from one place of experience to another. In each one the forces will have been given to him which he will be able to use through the exercise of mind and body in the mirror world. On earth the Universe is made known to us through the shining planets and stars, through the working of Sun and Moon. They are visible from outside. In the life before birth the soul has been within the living realm which he will afterwards see outside himself in the Heavens. To meet another person on earth is to see in him the signs of the world from which he has come. As he breathes, feels his heart beat, moves his limbs, knows the activity of his inner organs, he is feeling the after effects in himself of the Universe from which he has been sent out. Interwoven with them will be the character of the person which has been produced by his own human past. Supposing two people meet who feel in their hearts that they have known each other before, they are encountering in each other the after-effects and influences of the life in the Universe before birth. When furthermore they meet the past character of the one that each knew in an earlier time, they are looking at what has been transformed out of an earlier nature by the workings of divine justice through the will of great spiritual beings.

Reflecting upon the facts of the great area of experience that lies between birth and the death that has gone before, it is natural to realise what a vast difference there is in the person one meets today and the same individuality as one may have known him in earlier times. When the idea of reincarnation is contemplated on this level, one can think with awe of the immense transformation that the other person will have passed through, that one will have passed through oneself. Two human souls stand face to face who have been with the gods and have known their power to transform. Human souls coming back to earth again have been through worlds of experience since they were here before. Realistically speaking, the idea of reincarnation does not only imply other periods of experience on earth in other times, but also other journeys through the Universe.

Immortality

In the modern world ideas that were once known in the past and have been lost are coming back again. A phrase has been found,"life after life", for the question of the immortality of the soul. Centuries ago such a phrase would have been unnecessary, because everyone would have known that life does not cease at death, although there is profound change. In one of the stories of Chaucer from the history of the Canterbury pilgrims, in the one about Troilus and Cressida, the hero was killed. It is said that his friends, standing round the bier, saw the soul rising out of the body clapping his hands for joy at his release. Later on, only people with special knowledge would have known what in the fourteenth century was still evident to many. William Blake's drawing of the soul parting from the body at death was not generally recognised as real in his own time.

Within the meaning of history a good reason can be seen for the eclipse of the knowledge that the soul passes from one life into another. In the course of time changes of mind can be observed as they can likewise in the progress of an individual human life. Each change is related to the emerging of certain qualities and the dying away of others. In modern history it has been necessary for the experience of individuality to be developed. Its best fruit is observed when the individual person accepts responsibility for himself and his actions and behaves accordingly. Another way of putting this experience would be to say, "when I encounter a person who has a conscience which he values himself, then I have met someone in whom I have seen the up-to-date consciousness at its best." It has been a necessary condition through which state of mind could emerge to experience the importance of the single moment. To know that the present is the most important time, that it cannot be repeated, that it is the opportunity for me to act out of my own

conscience is the means through which the modern, responsible
state of mind can grow.

Much dark questioning has troubled many minds since the time
when the old knowledge was lost, as the power of natural second
sight declined. There have been struggles with doubt, there have
been the pains of unbelief and the terrible sense of loss which has
haunted those who could not realise that they would know their
loved ones again. The human mind has had to pass through tragic
struggles from which a certain kind of strength has emerged. It
is the strength of faith, not founded on tradition and teaching, but
on the discoveries of experience made by each person for himself.
When the idea of immortality comes to light again in the present
time, a new quality has been gained in the period during which it
was lost, hard though the process may have been. It is easier now
to think in terms of life after life than it has been for centuries,
although there are still those who cannot accept the thought of
immortality. Nevertheless, the one who nowadays looks within
himself, noticing the spiritual life which he finds there, becoming
aware of the essential core of his being as his individual spirit,
can know of himself that though human, he is an immortal soul.
He knows by experience. Feeling the unique opportunity of the
present moment, he will realise that it is also the seed of something
which will grow further in the life beyond the Gate of Death, that
he is responsibly involved now and also in the life to come.

Great as the transformation is between life in the body and
beyond it, the two states of experience, on earth and in the
Universe, are joined together by that which I make of myself.
My thoughts and my deeds will return to me in another form in the
life after death. My two destinies, there and here, will not be quite
separate, for the one will be woven into the other. Here during
the life in the body the human soul lives in the region of opportunities. In the hours of wakefulness the soul can change and bring
about change. Every day and in every hour of the day new beginnings can be made. They can be made in relationship to **myself**, to
what I think, intend and do, in relationship to other people and in
relationship to the worlds of spirit. What prevents this from being
realised in its true force are habits of mind within my own personality. It is hard to realise how little I am obliged to be fettered
by myself. I can in any hour say to myself, "Do I need to be as I
am, why am I thinking and behaving like this?" The grace given

by God to everyone while he lives here in the body on earth is the opportunity to change and to start again. At death this will cease. The soul will enter the region of consequences. He will encounter the experiences that belong to himself because he has prepared them, however little it may have been clear to him at the time. Experiences, heavenly and hellish, can be made by ourselves in the present time and will appear to us again as consequences when the other side of existence is made clear in the life after death. In passing through one life to the other, in leaving the earth for the Universe, the soul does not lose the pattern which he has known and helped to make here, so much as find it again to be lived through from the other side.

The process of seeing one's lifetime from the other side begins with a period of experience in consciousness. In the theology of an earlier epoch it was seen as Purgatory. Nowadays it should be seen with a difference. The soul is not exposed to a period of punishment for wrong. The human person is obliged to encounter the pattern of his experiences as it is seen in the Universe, as it is seen from outside, while on earth he knew it from inside. The other side of existence is as real and true as this side and is as much connected with the pains of regret and remorse as any encounter with repentance would be here. The pains of Purgatory are produced by a person himself when he beholds his behaviour with divine insight. What was once understood to be a period of punishment inflicted by divine power should now be seen as a pattern of consequences following justly upon one's own behaviour. Painful they must be, because this region of experience is that of consequences, unavoidable and morally justified. The pains of regret and remorse must be felt by the soul that they will bring about the wish to compensate for wrong done and great resolves for right to be done in the time to come. In this manner the painful encounter with consequences will become the starting point for new efforts to do well and to compensate for that which was unsatisfactory in the past.

When the soul has passed through the period of beholding consequences of the life before death, a process will begin of turning them into realities which have the power to form the character for the future. That will be built into the form of the coming time of the person who has himself brought about the consequences in a previous life on earth and turned them into forming influences for the future. Every human being is the result of the past which he has formed himself, but which has moulded his nature according to the forces of divine justice which work upon him after he has left the body. But within the life of the Universe he could only experience consequences. The region of opportunities has been left behind in earth existence. The soul can produce resolves for the future, but he cannot find the place in which to realise them except by returning to life in the body where the fact of opportunity exists. It is inevitable that this should be so. The Universe filled with the creative working of the will of God through the nine hierarchies of Heaven is the spiritual place where man can be re-made in terms of what he has made of himself previously, but it is no place for the exercise of his own will. He cannot transform himself or the situation in that region of consequences to which he goes at death. Only where he can live in the body, in the place of opportunity, can he transform himself and his destiny under the influence of the consequences that he has justly perceived.

Through such reflections it can be realised that reincarnation is part of the logical pattern of opportunity and consequence. The soul does not receive the urge to return to bodily existence out of his own feeling or desire, but through becoming aware of the urgent need to find opportunities to grow beyond the wrongs and weaknesses of the past and to give compensation for the events which they have brought about. Once the experience of the consequences has been transformed into resolves for the future, earth existence becomes the only place in the Universe where these urgent resolves can be turned into fact.

Earth existence within the pattern of the Universe is unique. . It is a kind of exception to all other conditions of life in other spheres. There are those to whom this is an unlikeable thought, who would wish to hear that there are other places of experience more important and more varied than that of the earth. Why not reincarnate in other planets? It is a question one often hears. According to the most external research into the character of other planets, none just like the condition of the earth has yet to be found. But might not that still be to come? But this is not logically to be expected, because the condition of the earth has to such a degree the character of an exception within the widths of the world. The physical size of the earth is no measure of its true importance within the Universe.

9

From the beginning of time the **Hierarchies**, through whom the will of God works, have brought forth the created world in all its wonders and have called in the powers of evil so to work upon it that the powers of God have been driven out. The earth is a beautiful memory of the will of God working at the beginning. But it is preserved in its present condition by the forces of death through which it is cut off from the other places of the Universe. But just the condition of death, balanced as it is by sufficient **forces** of life to prevent the earth becoming immediately a corpse, produces for mankind a place of existence where no divine power is at work to hinder the emergence of human will. Within the framework set by the laws of Nature, the human being can grasp and carry out intentions. A human person can thereby live independently of the powers of God for a time, until he meets them again on the other side of the Gate of Death. For a spell he is a being in his own right, a maker of his destiny, even the captain of his soul that the fruit may grow in him which shall be harvested out of the life of mankind on earth. Nowhere else but on earth are such conditions to be found. The curious may look for them, may hope to find them, but it is in the nature of things that their seeking will be disappointed.

Mortality

Which part of a person goes through the Gate of Death? What is left behind, what continues? In all considerations of the process by which the person of one incarnation becomes that of the next, that distinction should be faced which leads to recognising what is mortal in ourselves compared with what is immortal. The human being is put together, in a manner that can be studied in the work of Rudolf Steiner, out of three sheaths, or vehicles into which the eternal soul or spiritual Ego is implanted from above. The physical sheath is the body with all its substance of flesh which is prepared within the mother before the child's birth, and which should later become the temple of his spirit. Into such a reflection on human nature a differentiation should be introduced. There is only one manner in which the physical body in its own true nature can be really observed and that is to watch a corpse. The living body of a person is never seen alone without the forces of life which do not strictly speaking belong to it. A second sheath is related so closely to the physical that they are in the usual sense observed together. A body of life, living, moving, shot through with light and

10

shade, is the etheric sheath which overcomes the dead and heavy
qualities of the body that is purely physical. The substances of
the sheaths of both these kinds belong to the world of Nature. A
third sheath is composed of moving, living, coloured forces of soul
through which movement and function are present in the person in
whom all three sheaths work together. That is to say, the living
body is ensouled. In me and other people the person can be observed
in whom forces of soul, vitality and physical form, are interwoven.
The forces that are physical are known in the realm of Nature in
the mineral kingdom. The forces that promote growth, flowering,
fruiting and fading are revealed in the plant kingdom. The forces
of soul, producing movement and function, are manifested in the
animal kingdom. In the threefold bodily nature the person is related to the three kingdoms of the natural world with which he
lives on earth.

The spiritual part of a person, his Ego, is implanted into the
bodily sheaths in the course of the process of being born and
growing up. Whatever opinions may be expressed, no one seriously
identifies himself wholly with his physical body. He is inclined
to regard it as the means of being present, moving about and getting
things done. Little children are naturally inclined to regard the
body as a house in which the spirit takes up residence. In the
early years before schooling there is a natural tendency to draw
houses, because the children are experiencing so strongly their
efforts to build the growing house and learn how to live inside it.
The view that they draw these houses because they see them around
is contradicted by the experience that the first drawn houses
tend to follow the same pattern regardless of what the local housing
is like. The drawings represent inner experiences of the soul and
are not well related to that which can be outwardly observed.
Because the whole process is a living one, the house grows and
develops in relation to the spiritual being who lives in it.
Nevertheless, the person cannot be identified with his body.
Between soul and body the activity goes on which leads to consciousness. The forces of life from the vital body are involved
with growth, but likewise with the ability to form thoughts. The
soul body is the place where conscious experiences are recognised which arise because the forces of soul are reflected from
the mirror of the bodily nature. Are our thoughts thought with the

11

brain, or merely reflected from it? Is the brain an organ for the detection of the thoughts that live in the soul instead of being their producer? Because man is a spirit dwelling for a period in a threefold bodily sheath, the experience comes to him that he lives in spiritual activities about which he knows because they provide him with a mirror for his consciousness. Such considerations, enter into the reflections on which the mind dwells when thinking over the matter of reincarnation.

The sheaths are formed of mortal forces and are the mortal part of the human person. The Spirit is born immortal from the Universe beyond death. In the nature of a man the immortal and the mortal are woven together, only to be separated out at death. They bear each other company for the length of a lifetime. In so doing the Ego, or spiritual being, can absorb to himself some of the forces from the sheaths. These will then pass with the eternal soul into the life after death. All that shares the nature of the sheaths and is not united with the Ego goes through a process of dissolution, back into the spheres from which the forces within the sheaths have come. It is a matter of common experience that the substances of the corpse dissolve into the earth by the processes of decay or are dissolved by burning. The life forces of the vital body dissolve into a living Universe in a period that follows quickly on the death of the body. The forces of the soul body take a longer time to dissolve, but also return to the region of air from which they have come. These are the mortal remains which the eternal soul casts off at death.

It would be an illusion to hope that the portion of a human personality which lives reflected in body and soul could pass from one life on earth to the next. That which is mortal is dissolved away. A new mortal part is composed for the soul in the preparations for the new birth. One of the confusions that can arise in reflecting on the matter of reincarnation is the making of accurate distinctions between that which is mortal and immortal in the human personality, that is to say, between that which returns when the new life on earth begins and that which has been dissolved away at the the previous death. No one returns in a mortal sheath which he has worn before. It has been cast aside at death and the immortal soul has been clothed in new ones woven together out of the forces of soul life and physical substance fetched afresh from the world.

The manner in which the sheaths then appear is liable to be modified by the effect of the consequences experienced in the life between death and a new birth. But the appearance and personality of one life is not directly reproduced in the next. It can appear only in the influences that work through the consequences left over from the past. It is one of the dangers of the pictures produced by far memory that mortal elements can be confused with immortal ones. The changes between incarnations are liable to be much stronger and more decisive than such pictures suggest.

Destiny or Karma

How can one know about the hidden part of existence, about what happens in sleep and after death? A long time ago there was a widespread faculty corresponding to what is called second sight today. The hidden parts of existence were known in dream pictures, which have left behind a heritage in the old fairy tales and legends. They are full of wisdom well worth learning, but it is clothed in the language of pictures known to us today in dreams. In that early time of history the ordinary person was a dreamer, dreaming his life away. As the intellect developed as a general human faculty, the human mind woke up. The modern person is well-awake to his experiences on earth, but he has lost contact with the hidden part of existence, because he is no longer the dreamer. Psychologists of many schools put great value on the experiences in dreams and rightly so. But unless they are understood in waking life their language remains obscure and confusing. But today knowledge about the hidden experiences of the human soul has become something like a necessity if the great problems of existence are to be faced. It can become very clear to anyone reflecting on the question of reincarnation that he is being led into the area of these great and deep problems.

In modern times the thinker who has most scientifically, yet with spiritual integrity, widened the area of knowledge about the nature of man, is Rudolf Steiner. The ideas set forth in his work are treated here as real and true. This is not because he is being quoted as an authority, but because of a thought process which anyone may carry out for himself. His ideas have come into the world as discoveries just as we are accustomed to discoveries being made by atomic physicists, research workers in other spheres and technicians who invent machines. What we do with their ideas can also be done with those brought by Rudolf Steiner out of his research into the spiritual nature of the Universe. They can be tried out and experienced by ourselves and will be either confirmed or otherwise by the results. What hinders a person from making such experiments is more often fear than an inability to understand. There was a time, though it is hard to believe, when travellers by train dismounted in front of tunnels and walked over the hills to the other side. They were unable to trust the engineers who built them. Since then experience has shown that a train can usually travel safely through a tunnel. It has equally become accepted that most aeroplanes stay in the sky and reach their destinations, whatever the passengers may fear. Ideas that may be heard for the first time have to be trusted in the first place and they may gradually become a part of the life of the mind just as tunnels and aeroplanes are now part of our ordinary experience. Those ideas which have no real substance will tend to fade away into theories or dogmas. The true ones will become more real.

There have been religious people who believe that no thought should be given to the souls of those who have passed through the Gate of Death, because they had gone to God and God would understand. But those who believed this have put a barrier between themselves and the loved ones who had gone ahead by refusing to be concerned with them any longer. They have behaved like a certain lady whose husband had died after some years of an invalid existence. She complained that after the good nursing care she had given to him she had done her duty by the time he died and could hand him over to God. She was therefore annoyed when she found out that his presence was constantly with her and that he seemed to be asking her to think of him and to help him. She was unable to disbelieve in his presence, but she was filled with indignation that more was being asked of her than to do her duty up to the hour of death. But a new time of history has arrived. The human mind will not be left limited to the concerns which belong to the time between birth and death. It is appropriate that new ideas about the hidden part of existence should reach people just at the time when experience is being widened. It is worthwhile to encounter and consider them. There are pioneers on the path of spiritual knowledge just as there are pioneers in scientific and technical discoveries.

There is an exercise in biography which anyone who wishes to do so can make for himself. He can look back over his past and consider how the events of his life have come about and what they may signify. He may come to a better relation to his present and his future. Anyone who does this is likely to find that there is a pattern emerging from the pictures in memory which he has been observing. The pattern will emerge, not as something he has planned, but as something that really exists in his life and which he he has accepted. Such an exercise will lead to recognising that the term, "destiny" has substance. It means just this pattern which can be observed and in which the forces that determine the path of experience which each one takes are manifested. Such forces are then shown to be realities at work in our lives. If it seems that they compel us, it should be observed that the present decisions made by ourselves also work into the pattern and help to form it.

A human life can be looked at in the following manner. A person may look around and say to himself: certain forces are working into my life from the past, but there is an outlook towards the future within which my own thoughts and actions will have a strong effect. If the person is willing to look deeper into the realities, he can realise that he is standing between spiritual forces emanating from the spiritual places represented by the Sun and the Moon. From the direction of the Moon as a source of spiritual influences come all the effects that have been built up from causes in the past. The Moon is a spiritual place, in this sense, where that is preserved for the future which has been produced by an earlier personality. It is not carried by the eternal soul into the outer spaces of the Universe, because it could only be an hindrance. But what the Spirit of the Moon holds in store is to be given back later to the eternal soul and will work in earthly destiny as that from the past which has to be carried into the present. As often as not it will be experienced in sets of circumstances which a person can meet from time to time.

In childhood circumstances are mostly provided by parents. The father takes another job, makes money or loses it, decides to emigrate, or the parents separate and a one parent family is formed. From the angle of the children the pattern is being provided by the parents and has to be accepted. The autobiography of Golda Meir,

15

one of the foremost founders and leaders of the modern State of Israel, is a clear example. Her infancy passed in the South of Russia within an impoverished, endangered, Jewish family. Home was not a safe and happy place for her. Under the threat of persecution, her parents went to America and the children went too. Her scramble for education was experienced there and her early devotion to the idea of a homeland for her people. As a young woman with two children, she chose to leave America for a dangerous and uncomfortable life as a pioneer in Palestine. She no longer accepted circumstances, she produced them. Her own children accepted what was provided by herself, because they were still children. When they grew up they had a mother of great fame and influence in Israel. They could make themselves into devoted citizens or they could leave for America or other places in the world. In this manner the contrast in the lives of two generations can be observed between what is provided and what a person can decide to undertake himself.

The influences which work into the pattern to break up the necessities from the past and bring in choices for the future are directed by forces from the Sun. The person of today stands between the working of the Moon and the Sun, between necessity and opportunity, between acceptance and exertion. When he looks at the pattern woven by that which comes from the past, he can learn to understand and accept it as the situation from which the future begins. When he looks at his plans and purposes as that which he has not yet achieved, he can see for himself that the situation in which he is can be taken in hand, and transformed by his own efforts. In such a way he can find what is the pattern of his destiny and what he can intend to undertake.

How is the weaving of the pattern in destiny performed? The will of the human person is only part of the answer. The powers of God, working through the members of his being, the Angels, Archangels and all the Company of Heaven are the agents of destiny. An Indian word is often used for the process through which the pattern is produced when the will of God and the will of the person are interwoven. The word is Karma. It represents a living process which could be described, as it has been done here already, as a kind of moral digestion. That which flows out of the words and actions of a person into the world is gathered up into the life of the Beings of God and digested there to produce wisdom and goodness. That which falls away in unworthiness is rejected and in need of transformation. Consequences in this sense cause events and pressures which can be absorbed into the process of putting right what was wrong, and making strong what is weak. When the awareness of the human soul begins to share in the judgment of the Gods, the soul will become willing to cooperate with the urges of karma. They are directed towards compensating for harm done and learning under the pressure of experience to develop further in cultivating what is good and right. Karma could be described as education, through the encounter with just results and the need to compensate for wrongs done, towards a higher stage of human existence. It is a living process of forming destiny, involving the life of a single human being and groups of human beings. Harsh as some of its consequences may seem, the process by which karmic events come about is fraught with the wisdom of God and is directed by the aims inspiring human evolution. The working of karma is always wise and just. In our present time another influence of Grace can be observed coming into individual biographies. It can be looked for especially in the sphere where consequences are changed into new beginnings.

The process of karma can operate within one lifetime, but it appears most clearly and strongly where one life on earth is shaped from the effects of another in the past. Karma works most strongly between the lifetimes of the past and the present one. What has been said and done in one life passes through the moral processes of digestion among the Beings in the Heavens, who give it back again through the necessities and events of the later life. It has happened to me, why had it to happen to me? This is a query frequent among modern people. If the answer is available because the insight into the biography is sufficiently far-reaching, it can be observed that there is logic between cause and effect which can come only from the wisdom of God. In the areas of experience, where the wisdom and wishes of the single person operate, how easily errors and mistakes will appear. The modern person will look to develop the power of conscience, where decisions of his own are effective. He can look to learn by a wisdom greater than his own in the area in which he observes with wonder the wise workings of Karma. Of such value is the transformation in the person who leaves his life on earth, takes the sacred journey through the Cosmos and returns again to another life on earth, that the wise working of that Karma can only operate truly on the kind of scale which it offers. People need to encounter karma, that a greater wisdom than their own should prevail in the course of their lives. The gods need that the human soul should take the path through death into the Universe and again into birth, that their divine wisdom should be able to work into the process of man's evolving. People need the process of reincarnation that they may evolve towards the divine. The gods need it that they can work into the forming of true humanity within human souls. People need to return to the earth more than once and the gods need them to do so.

If I am to develop further as a human being, the wisdom of God will work upon me through the influences of Karma and I shall feel the urge to respond. I shall grow further in the interplay between what comes from the divine world and what comes from myself. Just as the seed in the ground responds to the beams of the Sun and grows upwards, so does the seed of my true humanity grow up in me in response to the divine wisdom shining through the events that form my destiny. The Hierarchies in the Heavens, the gods who work the will of God, are different from each other in their function. as they are different in wisdom and will. Only the highest of the nine ranks are powerful enough in wisdom to direct the weaving of karma, to form creatively the events which have originated in my past. Only they can live so powerfully in the divine righteousness, that they can bring forth the right patterns of destiny for the future. The human soul, passing from one life on earth to another and yet another, is directed by divine influences through the operation of karma. His different incarnations are given meaning in their relationship to each other by such wisdom. The influence of people on each other, the manner in which they help or hinder each other's development, is likewise given sense by the guidance from these wise spiritual powers of the Thrones, the Cherubim and the Seraphim. They are the highest ranks in the Heavenly community. They are the guardians of divine justice. They are the creators of the true pattern of man in man. Our future is not only the concern of ourselves. Our life is interwoven with their life. Our destinies are directed by their ideals. Without their interest and guidance, there would be no meaning in our existence, no significance in what happens to us. It is for us to develop a conscience of our own, that our ways may become nearer to their ways, our purposes to theirs.

Metamorphosis

The transformation from one life to the next was understood in
the past as a logic of cause and effect. With the coming of
Christianity another factor is to be considered. Some modern
psychiatrists have begun to believe that if they can envisage
experiences beyond those of this life, they can discover the
causes of the present suffering of their patients and intervene
more effectively. But if they think in terms of the old doctrine of
of reincarnation, they do not outgrow the familiar picture of past
behaviour and present results. The Christian factor enters in when
that which is developed for the future out of the present experience
is taken into the pattern: what is suffered today may have been
caused in the past, but faced with good will for the future, it can
be developed into the power to create what is to come. It can be
called the factor of resurrection. It is added by the working of
Christ to the old force, which brings about just consequences to
past causes. When it is possible, with tact and sympathy, to read
the biographies of other people instances of this working can be
found. A boy of eighteen lost his leg in the war. He was trained
in optics. In the course of years, in which the loss of his limb
was a great sorrow to him, an unusual skill developed in his fingers.
He had opportunities in medical research. He was able to live
long enough and to work hard enough to recognise that what he
had lost in his legs had come back to him in a skill of great value
in his unusual area of work. An example from an earlier piece of
history is found in the fate of a historian, who could represent the
spiritual influences at work in outer events with unusual conviction;
he was able to develop an unusual kind of historical imagination
under the conditions that he lived in through being totally deaf. Cut
off from many opportunities of communicating with people around
him, he developed his notable powers of historical understanding.
It may well have been that such people have been liable to become
victims of disasters because of that which belonged to their past.
What has grown in them of value for the future has developed out
of the manner in which the disasters were faced and their consequences transformed. If the one who says, "why did this happen to
me?" also says to himself, "what can I make out of this?", then
the new factor in human destiny, the truly Christian one, that which

has to do with resurrection, can be made real.

In the course of events described in the Gospels, something is spoken of again and again to which particular value was attached by Christ Himself. The word for it is faith. In situations of sickness or tragedy when (St. John Ch. 4), the Roman Centurion was mourning over his dying boy (servant or son), the outcome was decided by faith. Christ was carrying through the world of earth His cosmic power to create, His grace to bring new energy of spirit into human lives. The force of faith in the people who met Him drew towards them that which lived in Christ Jesus. The grace dwelt within Him, but of necessity it was curbed. By its own nature it flowed out to the lost, distressed multitude, but it was often restrained by divine effort, lest the whole world should be over-flooded and over-whelmed, lest the cramped old world should be split apart by the influx of divine splendour. But the curb could be released, the outflow set at liberty, when human hearts opened out in His presence to welcome in the divine power which was in His careful keeping. That which was set in motion when the heart opened in trust, was faith. It was in part insight, the willingness to comprehend, as the Centurion did, what was signified in the behaviour of Christ. It was likewise the warmth of heart flowing in confidence towards the sunshine of the spirit alive within Him. It was in great part will, to ask, to release by prayer, to call in the hour of need upon the bounty of His grace, that He might let it flow upon those who could seek and find. The Centurion could seem to say, ''I have beheld where it is that divine grace dwells. I have longed for it, and I have called it towards me in the hour of my need.''

In the meeting between the grace of Christ and the faith of the human heart, the wonder of metamorphosis is performed. When Jesus Christ walked by the Pool of Bethsaida (St. John Ch. 5), He gazed upon the cripples and the helpless ones assembled there in hope of cure. He spoke to one, to the man long paralysed, who was alone, who had not reached the water of the pool at the moment of healing. By His questions, He awoke in the sick man's heart the conviction that he was intent on being healed, that he was ready to change from the dependent existence of a cripple to the active one of a man fit for work. He healed him with the words, ''Arise, take up your bed and walk.'' The faith within the man pulled him upright. He had been lying down helpless for thirty-eight years. In one moment, the hour of the great decision, he stood upright. Reflecting on all that it means for someone to stand on his own feet, how the head points to the Stars, the feet are firm on the ground below, the arms can be stretched out into space, one can see that uprightness is the sign of proper selfhood. The one is helpless who lies down, he can help himself standing up. Egohood in the true sense was made real in the sick man when he arose.

He was instructed to take two actions after he had come to himself. He was first of all to lift up the bed on which he had been lying for so many years. According to the custom of the time, he had become an object of charity. All that he had for himself was the bed. It was in reality the token of his past. He was told to lift it up and carry it along. He had himself made the bed of suffering through the cause which had produced the paralysis, he had lain on it, he was to pick it up and take it with him. He had solved his problem and could carry it along. That done, he was to walk, to advance out of the past into the present and on into the future. He was to step out into the new decisions, the open opportunities that lay ahead.

The faith that changes situations can grow and live in the human heart because it is quickened by the grace of Christ. The divine powers that are working to form human destinies are the instruments of the justice of God. But Christ works with the unknown force of grace, the gift of the Son to augment the justice of the Father. He transforms the process of reincarnation by His creative touch.

From Past to Future

Reflecting on all that the idea of reincarnation implies, one may ask, "how great are the changes between one life on earth and the next?" It is a common experience to become aware that there are some people whom one seems to have known before and to be related to before the first encounter. Impressions of this kind are liable to misunderstanding and ask for careful consideration. But they can be indications of something real. They lead to the area in which the change in the well known person is also a matter of experience. In much of the modern literature on the subject this consideration can cause problems. Writers enjoying the romantic version of reincarnation have tended to discover the hero or heroine re-entering history at intervals with very much the same character from life to life. This provokes a very large question when the author seems able to accept repeated earth lives as a fact, but has left the idea of destiny or Karma out of account. At times the characters represented in this style seem to be repeating themselves from age to age of history and becoming unable to emerge from the same round of relationships. To awaken to the mysteries of reincarnation involves becoming more aware of how the will of God works into human affairs. It means contemplating God's point of view. To say this might seem to put the whole matter into a religious context. This in fact it does, for the whole process of birth, death and re-birth is not credible without the influence of divine wisdom. It is as much and more beyond the range of human imagination as the emerging of the flower from the sprouting seed or the moving of the Stars on their intricate courses. Of all the wonders of the created world that of the course of a human destiny is the most mysterious. The imagination so easily falls short that disbelief can be the easiest course to take.

Imaginative thinking can grow and develop in the mind with practice. The work of Rudolf Steiner is of particular value because it gives the opportunity to develop the powers with which to understand the ideas put forth there. Anyone who takes up one of his books to read carefully can discover that he is being offered new realities to consider, but equally, lines of thought that will lead him to them. He therefore by thinking them is never using his mind under authority. He finds that the power to understand grows with thinking. But he will never be spared the need to think for himself and to exercise his powers of imagination.

The process of change from life to life is described as one in which soul becomes body. The psychological outlook of one lifetime will form the bodily constitution of the next. That which seems in the present to have been thrust upon one will turn out to be a condition that the person of the earlier incarnation has formed himself. Naturally, the present person does not always agree with the person he once was. But this can happen also between youth and old age in one lifetime. Experimenting with some of the knowledge from his work, such examples as these can be produced for consideration. There are two kinds of people, as the psychologist Jung frequently pointed out. There are those whose interest goes out strongly to the world around them and those who

22

turn readily inwards to the life of their own mind. Everyone, up to
a point, can move in both directions and knows by experience where
they lead. The person who in one life turns his interest outwards
prepares for himself wirey, curly hair in the next. His hair springs
later as his feeling sprang earlier. The person inclined to contem-
plation in one lifetime prepares fine, straight hair for the next. The
hair lies against the skull as the thoughts lay in the mind. These
are the two extremes between which the great variety in the growth
of hair is to be found. Nowadays, fashion intervenes. Why do
the Europeans favour wavy hair to the point of producing it mechan-
ically? Why do Africans take the trouble to have their hair straight-
ened?

It can be observed that at a certain stage in childhood, often
between seven and ten years old, the eyesight will take on the
character which will persist in later life. The change may be sudden
and violent, or gradual. That which has come from the cast of mind
in an earlier life will express itself in the present one as the child
emerges from the strong influences of heredity. Long sight expres-
ses the interest in the world of an earlier person; short sight ex-
presses the interest in the inner world of the one who went before.
Those with balanced sight will be those who commanded common
sense at an earlier time, those with diverse sight in the two eyes
will reflect dramatic changes in the course of a previous lifetime.
If one looks back and pre-supposes the previous life within the period of the Middle Ages, or earlier, it is not difficult to imagine how
such results could come about. There have been in the past times
in history when people were divided socially into two types. There
were those who tilled the soil or fought the wars, religious people
most likely, but following their duties in the external world. There
were those, held to be equally important at the time, devoted to
religion and the practice of prayer, whose inward activity was of
value to all the others. Still others found a balanced way, giving
equal value to both. At the same time it often happened that the
change from one extreme to another was made in one lifetime.
The warrior would spend his last years in the monastery, the
pilgrim would settle down at home. The one who failed would retire
from the world. All such influences in one life will have formed the
constitution of the next. That which is of the soul has turned into
the nature of the body.

Such a thought can induce understanding for the sufferings which
beset many people. It is unnecessary to look upon them as punish-

ments. They are consequences which should be transformed for the sake of the future. In the past a person could not always defend himself against the force of circumstances produced by the people around him. Not everyone who took up the religious life chose to do so out of his own sense of vocation. His place in society would have been chosen for him. There are those today with problems that might well have come because too many years of the previous life were spent in the monastery or convent, which that person may have never wished to enter. Others will be carrying the after effects of a life devoted to vows taken before they understood what was meant. How many of those who went on the crusades in Mediaeval Europe knew how far away the holy places in fact were and in what they would be involved in trying to get there? How many people of those times were caught up in passionate religious impulses, whereas today they would be caught up in materialistic ones. Nevertheless, the activities with which people were involved in the the past had in themselves healthly consequences. The mower mowed with his scythe, the ploughman ploughed with his horses, the blacksmith hammered on an anvil, manuscripts were written by hand, clothes were sewn, seamen rowed their boats and trimmed their sails. So much hard work involved movements of the limbs, which can build up heads for the future. Nowadays, there is much saving of labour, much reliance on machinery, but what will be the consequences in future times of the lack of activity to which the wonderful machines contribute? What is the difference made by the kind of activity, involving forces of feeling and will, which are experienced today compared with those of former times, the consequences of which maintain us in our modern form?

Knowing about reincarnation and some of the principles which are at work in its process should have an effect upon the forming of the impulses of conscience today. Interesting knowledge should have its consequences in behaviour. One hears it said quite casually that what I do not have this time I can hope for in the time to come. Or, further opportunities for what I want will be in store. In reality the inter-weaving between one life and the next does not take place on the surface but in the depths of the human heart, where the moral impulses work strongly. What a person has hated this time, he may seek out in the next life simply by force of the previous antipathy. The voice of the conscience could warn against passionate feelings of racial and national discrimination, against fostering dislike and grudges, because they will inevitably pass from the region of feeling into the outer realities of destiny in another life. Considering the effect of one's actions requires much more moral imagination when it is realised that the consequences will reach much further than the present and return in a new form in the future. What I make of my life now I shall find again much further ahead. To take an interest in the idea of reincarnation is to involve oneself with greater and greater problems of conscience.

Man's Place in History

What would a person be without his past? His memories stretch back to the time in early childhood when he began to form conscious pictures of what had happened. That which he cannot recall still lives on in him nevertheless, at a less conscious level, and emerges in his behaviour. Memories of this kind will reach still further back into the past, gathering proofs of experience from before birth and from earlier times of existence in the world of earth. All such memories, far and near, fuse together to fashion the person as he is now. In some people the fusion is more harmonious than in others. Some break with their past, carrying bits and pieces around with them, while others can weld together the whole personality. The integrated person is the one with his past well in hand.

It is the same with mankind. A family, a city, a nation, a country has a past fused together into its history. The family has keepsakes and pictures, the city or nation monuments in which the past continues to be remembered. Each single person is placed through the forces of destiny within the history of such groups and their memories influence his personal ones. The child as he grows up, has to learn about the past of his family, the place in which he resides, the country to which he belongs and, if he is to develop proper width of mind, of mankind itself because he is human. But history has to be made as much as it has to be learnt. Each person is a history-maker in his own right. The experience of so being is fraught with difficulties nowadays. The societies of today are organised in so impersonal a manner that it is hard for the single person to feel effective. It seems to himself that he suffers under history more than he makes it. Nevertheless, this is really an illusion.

In the region of history there is much at work today to produce illusions. Wise remembrance of the past requires thought and even study. Versions of what has been can be put about with the aim of spreading untrue pictures, with intentions good or bad. Recently hoardings for advertisements were apt to carry the representation of a row of figures. At the start was an ape-like, crude creature. At the end was an upright human form. In between were a series of other figures in transition from one extreme to the other. The whole was intended to show in brief the history of Man. The passer-by could take it or leave it, but he could easily become the victum of illusion. If he did not consider the matter saying," is it true, why take it on show? ", he could assume it to be a real picture of Man and his past. To liberate himself from such an illusion he would have to give the matter thought.

History is much exposed to manipulation today, because as a person believes his human past to have been, so he is apt to make his mental pictures of the future and the aims of his actions will be influenced. If he is to be directed to fulfilling the aims of his government, in school or in the press, an appropriate view of history will be presented, even if it contradicts known facts. Is there no way into true history? There is a faculty of the heart which can be called goodwill for the realities, which guides the mind. It disperses illusions and opens the way to recognising what is true. It promotes learning from experience. It sharpens observation. But it is not an easy way out, because it demands questioning and striving to think further.

There is another way of knowing history besides reading or hearing about it and that is being part of it. The inner sense of reality is fed in our minds by forgotten experiences of the past. They reach back in former epochs of time when the ''I'' that I still am was on earth before in other personalities. In the broadest sense, the history of Man is my biography. I have been involved with it in two ways. Either I was on earth and helping to make it by my beliefs and actions, by what I joined in or avoided. Or I was on the pilgrimage through the regions of the Stars looking at the events on earth from outside, learning with more percipience or less, as an onlooker. I participated in the whole history of the world, sometimes more vividly than at others. But at all times the life of Mankind was my life and my separate life was woven into the whole. Each single person can trace the course of his individual destiny when he looks

back down the avenue of his past. But it is set into the landscape
of history. Other paths of separate destinies cross with his. His
family has a destiny, the nation to which he belongs, the country
in which he lives and works. He may have been born into one
nation and spent much of his life in a country which is not the
nation's homeland. A large part of the world's population is on
the move today, whether or not by choice. In all these areas of
life single destinies are interwoven with those of groups and all are
within the pattern of Mankind's destiny.

Epochs in History

Epochs of time have characters of their own which likewise influence the character of each person. If I had lived one hundred years
ago, what would my life have been like then? What outlook would
have been natural, what would I have been likely to undertake?
Where would my interests have lain? It is not only the inventions
of this century that alter my experience. There are ways of thinking,
attitudes of mind, philosophies that appear today which would not
have been in existence. The single person joins in the trends of
thought just as much as in the events of his day. I am a person of
history in my own right.

I carry the past of Mankind in myself as I do my own because I
have lived it. I have been, as we all have been, enveloped in the
soul-consciousness of the ancient Indian Epoch. I knew then what
it was to depend on the divine forces of the Heavens instead of the
natural ones of the earth. My soul recognised itself as Star born,
wandering on earth an exile, a homesick one beset with misgiving,
turning fervently to the lost gods. I have been, as we all have,
clothed in the soul-consciousness of the ancient Persian Epoch.
The sense of duty, of piety towards the earth awoke. The gods
dwelt in the Heavens, but their revelation was on earth. To labour
in the soil, to revere the cycle of life, sowing, growing, harvesting
and fading were holy experiences. The exile went to work. Life
on earth showed a new meaning. Piety was divided, flowing towards
the gods but likewise towards their working in nature on earth. The
exile became involved in the struggle between darkness and light,
between the Princes of Evil and Good. The urge to withstand, to
overcome, to solve the conflict, developed and spread. The image

of the Heavenly Champion withstanding the powers of the adversary emerged.

I have been, as we all have, wrapped in the old Egyptian consciousness. Whether or not anyone actually lived by the Nile, or whether he felt the Egyptian influence in another land, he still bears today hidden memories of the time when the wisdom about the earth, the Heavens and Man, had that character. Osiris, the god of the Sun on earth, was dismembered by the dark god Set, and rose again in the land of Amentis, the king among the dead. The sorrowing widowed goddess of the Moon, Isis, bore the son Horus, through whom the gods could still speak. The human soul, still an exile, became active and conscious of himself on earth. He could find his way back to the world of the gods in the Heavens in the hard pilgrimage through death into the Judgement Hall of the gods. There he had to show what he had made of himself in human life on earth and so gain or lose admission to the kingdom of Amentis.

In the Graeco-Latin period the classical cast of mind will have been mine as it was that of everyone. By that Epoch the one-time exile had become at home on earth. He erected fine temples to the gods to give them a welcome in his world. They were truly his companions, their shrines were at the centres of cities and on the loveliest heights of the countryside. They came and went between the Heavens and the earth. But when the time came for the souls of men and women to approach the gate of death, they felt themselves sucked down into the dark, into the unwelcome world of shadows. They had become real to themselves on earth. They had loved and worked there with the divine sources of souls and body which the gods had given them.

Since the close of that Epoch, I have lived, we all have, with the powers of consciousness that have developed within us, in contrast with those which have declined because they reached the soul from outside through the divinity in nature. Nowadays we tend to believe that our human selves have taken over history. It is not the fashion at present to remember the mighty cosmic beings who blow the winds of change and breathe the urges into the epochs of time as they come and go. And yet they are at work still. But the situation of man on earth in the universe has in fact been changed, not by his own will but by the descent of the Son of God from the heavens into earth existence. The coming of Christ, the overcoming of death, the new beginning of the Resurrection make up the turning point of man's evolving. History did not bring them forth. History has been invaded by the divine world above. The future will depend on how this event is received into our souls, on how we understand and know it. To face this, to feel the spirit within ourselves, which is the seed planted by Christ in our hearts, is our present responsibility.

If each person has knowledge of this hidden within him, if each soul is the repository of the memories of human history, even if they are too big for his consciousness, how did he actually come by them? Many views are expressed about how often a soul reappears in the body in terms of reincarnation. The best informed view is that of Rudolf Steiner. Through his research into the realities of history, he anticipated that about a thousand years of time on earth would pass between one incarnation and the next. That would be the regular pattern, although exceptions can come about. That would mean about two appearances of each one within each epoch of the type which has already been outlined. That is to say, that each person will have had two opportunities to take part in and gather memories of such periods of history. The gaps of time may sound long, but it should be realised that for a human being to be re-constituted in the Universe for another existence in the body is a mighty undertaking. One little boy, who seemed to know something by experience, called it "hard work for God".

In our present age some variations in the general pattern may well be taking place. The processes of time show signs of speeding up. Special problems of character may have to be faced in consequence. Some souls may be asked to carry exceptional burdens of history out of line with their own development. Now that Mankind has to become so self-dependent in the conduct of his evolution, new undertakings may well be required. Not for nothing has Christ shared a portion of His creating Spirit with Man. Each one of us is differently involved in the making of history thereby.

Our present age lies within the fifth of the great Epochs that followed the decline of Atlantis. We struggle with the emerging force of the ego, of that in the human soul which is individual spirit. In the course of history, the single person emancipates himself from the group, from race, nation, tribe, even from the family, to become an independent entity. There is the danger that the one on his own may become the victim of selfishness, retiring in upon himself, or falling into conflict with those around him in a war of all against all. There is likewise the opportunity that he will become heroic, disciplining his inner nature until he becomes master of himself and can be devoted to great purposes within the history of Mankind. All modern people live in such a situation.

Archangels

In the urges that work in the different ages of time, the influence can be traced of those beings of the Universe usually termed the Hierarchies. In an old description they are called, Angels, Archangels, and all the Company of Heaven. They are the invisible, real authors of God's creation. Some of them in a certain rank direct epochs of time, giving them a particular character, each of which impresses itself upon those who live at that period. "The strong wind blowing the new direction of time." (D.H. Lawrence), is a reality stemming not from people but from beings of the Universe working to inspire human progress. The one among them most to the fore in our present history is the Archangel Michael. He is the valiant one who fights the dragon that would devour in us the true image of Man. He calls to Mankind to face what has become evil in the impulses of our nature and to lift the heart towards the aims for the future that live in Christianity. He shows in our history how really people and societies can destroy themselves by giving way to violent urges within them and how urgently they need to find the means of transforming themselves.

Changing Destiny

When today groups have the drive to express themselves it is often through gangs that wreck each other, in mobs that want to tear apart those that they are against, in the miseries produced by terrorists. The old kind of adherence to tribe or nation has gone to the bad. The individual, instead of seeking support from the group, has to become capable of giving where in the past it was the custom to receive. He needs to become so much the part of the destiny of Mankind that he can give influences of progress to the world of his time. In terms of reincarnation this carries with it the kind of duty to move from one national group and kind of society to another, from one earthly life to the next. It is very exceptional if an individual soul comes more than once into the same group. It puts him into the danger of being influenced too deeply by that kind of character. There is an urge in everyone to move through the world from one group and countryside to another with the aim of learning over the spaces of time how to be part of all Mankind, how to gather the whole of history into oneself. In the person who has shown goodwill to the group in which he has passed an incarnation and to the generation in history to which he has belonged, the urge to go elsewhere next time can have a healthy outcome. But should anyone attack or despise other groups because of the one in which he stands himself, he will inevitably project himself towards the hated or misused group next time. Violent antipathies are a mistake in the present and a menace in the future.

The forces directing destiny from one lifetime to the next will naturally guide the individual soul away from what is one-sided towards the opportunity for varied experience. So it comes about that the individual needs to know what it is like to live both as a man and a woman. Usually the two types of incarnation will alternate, the individual being a woman, if he has been a man last time, and a man if he has been a woman last time. There are exceptions but they can bring great problems into the experience of the individual. It is likely moreover that the soul will be led to very different kinds of work, status in society and type of experience. Someone who was an intellectual in one incarnation would want to help himself by using his limbs more than his head in another. He could only become weaker by following frequently the main bent. In the same manner the one who has lived with greater outer activity is likely to look for greater opportunities of inward effort later on. Furthermore, the one who has played a large part in outer history in one lifetime will be directed into a more obscure destiny afterwards, for his forces of energy will have been depleted. Historically there is such a thing as "a rest incarnation". This is not to be understood as a time of no activity, but as an opportunity to build up reserves of power and strength for future responsibility in another lifetime.

It will usually be observed that in the course of a single destiny there will be times of disappointment, even of frustration that may or may not be produced by oneself. Promising situations will fall apart, the job, the journey, the human relationship that has begun does not mature. Those with powers of endurance will plod along, even under the weight of disappointment, others may break down. There is another process at work behind the scenes. That in a lifetime which comes to fruition, which brings outer success and

31

gives satisfaction to the one concerned, is exhausted in the process. That which is held back and restricted from coming to fruition has in it the seeds of the future. That which could not be expressed is saved up and can be taken into the life after death to be the seed of something new and greater for the time to come. Much depends upon the inner energy to hold fast to the aim within the individual soul. The human soul lives in alternations between resignation and prosperous expression of his aims. He will feel strength from the satisfaction of aims fulfilled, but he will be sent on his way with a treasure for the time to come from his disappointments and failures. To live in the awareness of long rhythms of time, to know that the present isn't everything, can be to cultivate a deeper wisdom in the experience of the present life. Everyone is a person in the present, but he is destined to become another kind of person in the future. He gathers his harvest, but he sows his seed and often enough the tragedies of his life will bring forth the best seed for the future.

Reincarnation in the Gospels

The Bible reader will naturally want to ask where reincarnation is to be found in the New Testament. Are we to suppose that the idea lives in the mind of the founder of Christianity and his followers? The Gospels are sayings of records and doings, they tell of the revelations of Christ, without much in the way of explanation or philosophy. There is no discussion about the existence of God. He is, and his mind is made known more fully through the teaching of Christ. Heaven and earth are, and their relation is described but not explained. The Father has sent the Son to earth. That is a matter of history. The gospels are to be read on their own terms. How many modern readers would not have wished to find proofs for the existence of god, evidence for the survival of the soul in the life after death, an explanation of the existence of evil. But the words of the Gospels speak of realities, which, it is supposed, everyone sees for himself, but which are deepened by the comments of Christ Jesus. The parable of Dives and Lazarus (Luke, Ch. 16, v. 19-31) says that people will meet after death the consequences of their behaviour here on earth. The consequences will be as real on the other side of the gate as the causes are here. He was speaking to people who were aware that the gate of death opens on to a real existence, they did not need to be told. The parables of Tares or Weeds (Matthew 13) sown in the wheat field by night assumes that the householder has an enemy who wants to ruin his field on the sly. To the servants who ask where the weeds come from, he replies,"an enemy has done this." Then he instructs them, in the treatment of the evil weeds. To save the good plants from harm, the weeds should be left, until they are separated from the harvest. God has sent out the sower (Matthew 13) to sow new seed of spirit into man's life on earth. We know that God is, because the seed is sown. When it is accepted that this is the style of the gospels, and that they are intended to be so composed, then it becomes realistic to look for the way in which the idea of reincarnation is present in the same manner.

John the Baptist

There are two passages which are constructed upon this idea and have no meaning without it. There is no explanation nor exposition of it as a belief. But the matters quoted already are also not quoted in that way. The first of these passages is about the character and mission of John the Baptist. It is to be observed in the Gospel of St. Luke that his birth followed a particular pattern, indicating an important task in history. He was the child of parents too old for childbearing and childless until that time. He was marked for holiness from the beginning. He was guided by the guardian spirit of his people for a purpose. He was born to be the herald of the Messiah for Whom it was the task of Israel to provide the right kind of body. John grew up to follow the way of living of the order known to history as the Essenes, to themselves as the true sons of Zadok, to us in modern times as the men of the desert whose library of scrolls was hidden in caves near the dead sea. The characteristics of his life styles pictured in the gospels are those of this order of ascetics, who devoted themselves entirely to awaiting the expected Messiah. The simple rough garment, the poor diet, are true to type. But whereas the Essenes dwelt in settlement and worked together, John went out alone into the wilderness in the manner of a hermit, contemplating incessantly the great vision of the One who was to come. The vision waxed so powerful, that he was driven by the urge to preach, to warn those around him of the world drama into which the world would be drawn. Great crowds were so moved by his outcry that they flocked to him with urgent questions about how they should prepare themselves for the coming hour.

John the Baptist was the most revered character of his time. The prophets of old had long ceased to speak, but he appeared like one of them, come again, to his listeners, who felt the force of his words sear their hearts. He awakened their longing to find a way to be saved, from the great catastrophe which they dreaded but which was in reality the world-event for which their forefathers and they themselves had long been hoping. A conflict of feeling broke the hearts of those who met John, the great longing which had been passed down the generations of their people, at odds with the dread of facing the One whose advent might bring upon them a last judgment or so they had been warned. The preaching of John had in fact an entirely strange message, in contrast to that which they had been taught of old. To be children of Abraham was to mean nothing in future, but it had been and still was for many, the strongest hope of rescue. "God is able of these stones to raise up children from Adam to Abraham", cried John, shattering the strongest belief of a good Jew at a blow. "Even now, the axe is laid to the root of trees", he continued. However much he shattered his hearers they followed him the more. "If our old hopes are void, what then shall we do?"

The good Israelite of the time would have expected to hear that the Law of Moses was his protection, that he who did not sin against it was secure. John the Baptist in his answers to his excited listeners never, according to the gospels, spoke of the law. Historically it is one of the most extraordinary features of his behaviour, considering that he was the latecomer to the prophets It speaks loudly to the power of his presence and his preaching that he carried his hearers with him. He spoke to them in terms of their own conscience. They were to judge how a taxgatherer or a soldier had to behave in his job to do rightly. John gave very simple advice, but it appealed to something in his hearers, which was only just emerging into the changing human mind. Later on, in the Sermon on the Mount, Jesus Christ was to make the matter plain. He spoke of the law, and of the pattern of behaviour which it required. But he went on to contrast this with the inner state of the heart which produces behaviour (Matthew 5). "You have heard that it was said, that you shall not kill. But I say to you that everyone who is angry with his brother shall be liable to judgment." John the Baptist had already spoken to his followers about the attitude of mind out of which they should behave. He had already preached about the change from law without using the word itself.

John spoke powerful words to the people, but he added the holy
action of Baptism by Water. In so doing he was not following
any tradition known in the Old Testament. The sacred washings
practised in the order of the Essenes must actually be the origin of
the ritual which John performed. On the site of the settlement of
Qumram, the large water tanks can still be seen required for the
ceremonies of purification. John took up the rite and carried it to
the ordinary people outside. They went through the decisive crisis
of a lifetime, when at the Baptism each was held under the water, to
the stage at which drowning was near. In the state of consciousness
induced by this condition, their souls beheld that which reflected their
own past, that of the chosen people and that of mankind. In that experience of the effect of the fall into evil,   the danger of death to
the human race was realised, and gave the shock through which the
souls could turn to what was to come.

The greatest event in the mission of John, was the Baptism of
Jesus. Not one of the crowd, but One whom he recognised as more
significant than all others, came to the banks of the Jordan to ask
for Baptism. John said, "You should rather baptise me." But Jesus
knew that John was he who was sent to perform the Holy act, by which
the purpose of his own life would be fulfilled. In the rite of Baptism
that took place through which the spirit of Christ entered into the
living soul and body of Jesus. It was a death-process for Jesus, a
birth process for Christ. That happened, which never before or since
could be repeated, that the spirit of the Logos itself, began to dwell in
a human form, began to partake in human existence on earth. Thereby
the evolution of man in the world reached its turning point. That
which had so long been a descent, became at Golgotha, an ascent.
The human way to the future began to be that which shall lead onward
and upward to realms of the Father.

All and everyone who met John would have been willing to receive
him as the promised Messiah, but he refused. To their question (John
One) he answered, "No ". He was the voice in the wilderness. Jesus
Christ was the Word in human form. He was the herald to the One
greater than he, who was to come. But when Jesus Christ was asked
about John (Matthew 11), he answered, "for all the prophets and the
prophets and the law prophesied until John, and if you are willing to
accept it, he is Elijah who is to come." To those who reject the
thought of reincarnation within Christianity, these words may seem
symbolic. As Elijah worked in his own time, so John works now - such

a saying would mean. But to those to whom the idea of reincarnation can be understood, in a Christian sense, these words mean quite simply that Christ was declaring that the present John had once lived a lifetime as Elijah.

Moses and Elijah were considered to have been the two pillars of Israel in whom the mission of their folk was fulfilled. Elijah struggled valiantly for the faith of Jehovah against the threat that the fascination of other faiths would bring the Israelites to lose their mission. Especially he had to face the conflict with Jezebel, the foreign queen who imposed the religion of the beautiful god, Baal. Elijah was persecuted by Jezebel, just as later on John suffered even to his death by beheading under Herodias. Elijah fought; John proclaimed with fiery strength. But Elijah came as a lonely outcast to the high hour of his destiny as a prophet. An event happened on the Holy Mount Horeb. The Lord God had promised the revelation of Himself. Behold, a whirlwind rose on the mountain, but the Lord was not in it. An earthquake shook the mountain but the Lord was not in it. A fire burned over the mountain side, but the Lord was not in it. At last, Elijah heard the still, small voice. In that hour, history changed. There awoke in the inner place of the human soul awareness of the indwelling spirit. That which had worked powerfully upon people from outside was known as an inner presence. In this event the coming of Christ was prepared, the time was to come when He was to say, "The Kingdom of Heaven is within you."

Elijah prepared the coming of Christ in the prophetic experience sent to him on Mount Horeb. The birth of the human Spirit within the soul came about in him which would be fulfilled after the death and resurrection of Christ, which St. Paul described as "not I, but Christ in me." Elijah was the herald of His coming within human history, John became the herald of His outer coming into history. What began within became an outer reality. In this sense it can be understood that Christ was speaking about a real process of reincarnation, when he said of John, "This is Elijah".

The Man Born Blind

The second instance of repeated earth lives being manifested in the Gospels is in Chapter Nine of the Gospel of St. John. It is a matter there of a man born blind met on the road side. The disciples are said to have asked who had sinned, the man or his parents. How could the man have sinned in the sense of that question, except in another lifetime? The disciples were thinking along the lines that the wrong of one life can be the affliction of the next. The habitual liar will develop later, a weak physical body (Rudolf Steiner). Suffering shows itself later in beauty, grief in bountiful vitality. Especially in regard to the sense of sight, the change from life to life shows itself. The person of limited outlook in one lifetime can develop short sight later. The broad outlook will become long sight. The balanced state of mind can bring even sight. The disciples must have been aware of such processes to have put the question as they did. It makes no difference to the matter that the answer of Jesus Christ was in the mysterious saying that neither the blind man nor his parents had sinned, it was a matter of the works of God being made manifest in him. Jesus Christ did not reject their question in the form in which it was put. He acknowledged it, and therefore all its implications, but he pointed out that the secret of the question was to be found in the future, not in the past. There was more to come in this man's life than had yet come. The disciples, like many other since who have looked at the matter in terms of karma or destiny had been seeking for an explanation in the past. The thought of living in earth existence more than once is closely interrelated with that of human destinies woven into patterns inspired by divine wisdom. The word 'karma' is mostly used for this thought. To contemplate reincarnation apart from the weaving of destiny is to form a concept without meaning in the spiritual sense. What purpose can there be in returning repeatedly to earth if there is no development in relationships between people, no progress of the self? How can there be development without destiny, and the wise working of karma? Nevertheless, that which flows from the past into the present appears in the form of necessities, of effects produced from previous causes. This is not all that takes place in human affairs.

In the story of the man born blind, Jesus Christ had shown that something more flows in from the future to meet what comes from the past. Opportunity meets necessity. The man has been born blind and is still blind. In the custom of the times, he must have been a beggar, living on the charity of his pious neighbours, not having the status of a responsible citizen. Jesus Christ did not ask about the man's past. He spoke of the spiritual power of Light within Himself. He then set about healing the blind man by a process involving several stages. He made an ointment, clay from the ground, mixed with the substance from his own body, spittle. The man's eyes were anointed. He was instructed to bathe in a famous pool of fresh water. The healing power of the water was added to the clay from the ground. To find his way to the pool while still blind, he must have asked for the help of other people, neighbours. It would have called for activity on his part, speaking to ask for help, walking to arrive at the pool, washing when he had come there. Out of the process in its varied parts came the climax of the actual healing. A blind beggar became a new seeing person.

This is only the beginning of the story, as it is told in St. John's Gospel. The true significance of the gesture of Christ towards the future appears in the next, longer portion of the account. The blind man began to see inwardly as much as outwardly. He was a passive figure, before; he became a person with an ego, with the means of intelligence at his service. During the inquiry into his healing both by the neighbours and the authorities, he proved able to exercise more and more inner powers of light, to stand up for himself at the climax for the one who had healed him. He had to stand alone, his parents had cast him off in fear. Those in authority bullied him. He found the best of answers to their questions but in spite of this he was cast out of the community to which he belonged for refusing to change his loyalty to the healer. He upheld the One who had healed him with wit and courage. In his loneliness he met Jesus Christ again. His inner eyes were opened to recognise that he had met the Messiah. The process of learning to see was then fulfilled. He attained first to outer sight, then to the sight of the mind, and lastly to the spiritual insight to see, and know, Christ.

None of this could come from the direction of the past. The light of Christ falling upon this man's life was grace. In grace came the opportunity to be reborn from the light in body, soul and spirit. To this man who had fallen into darkness, his loss of sight was a starting point. The end was that someone was entirely reborn in grace. The working of karma can become the means of working out of the past, even for compensating for what has been done and said. But to be reborn in the pattern of wholeness asks for the operation of grace, for that which shines from the future into the present. It is spoken of in the gospel, in the phrase, ''the works of God shall be made manifest.''

Evolution and Resurrection

Evolution has been a fact of history long before it became a theory. The word has been taken over by the followers of Darwin for worse rather than for better. In itself its meaning is much wider and more comprehensive. The reader of the Bible finds himself faced with a worldwide picture of Man's evolving history. It is based on facts and events that have happened. It is quite apart from any theory. It was in reality not until the nineteenth century that the human mind became ready to grasp evolution as a principle, although it had always been a fact of experience. Just as it was a long time before people in Europe could face the concept that the earth is round, although it has always in fact been round, so it was a long time before the concept of moving, evolving history could be grasped, although it had always been a reality.

The pattern of history described in the Bible begins with the creation of Man and his world by God. The image of Man is the image of God at the beginning. The worlds of Heaven and Earth are the same. Man's life is pictured in the same harmony as the stars have among themselves. God-given, star-born Man was created innocent and at one with the Creator. Into the untroubled childhood of Mankind a disturbing influence was introduced. In the Bible it is said that into the Garden of Paradise the serpent crept and no heavenly power came forward to eject him. Entirely at one with all the creatures around them, the first human souls had no means of distinguishing the serpent from the other creatures. They had been born without the means of saying no. The Divine warning against disobedience could scarcely have been comprehensible to those who had only known obedience. Through such pictures in the Book of Genesis the great fact of the fall of Man into evil has been described. Even for those who do not read the Bible, the fact of existence is unavoidable and constantly to be experienced. Every time anyone begins to do something which falls short of his own expectations when it is done, he has encountered his fallen nature. Every time anyone finds himself saying and doing that which he afterwards regrets, he realises that his human character is flawed. Being human, he aims at what he cannot achieve, he disappoints his own expectations, he is a less satisfactory person than he would like to be. Whether or not one accepts the picture in the Book of Genesis as valid, in the language of daily experience the saying is being constantly confirmed that Man fell into the grip of evil very early in his history. This is the decisive fact that has followed upon the original one, of the creation.

Fallen Man

The whole first half of the Bible - the Old Testament - is the history of how the event of the Fall, initiated by the serpent, developed through

the generations. It is the history of the decline and fall of Man.
The great heroes, the leaders of God's people, are shown as also the
inventors of new sins. After the appearance of such good men as
Abraham and Isaac, Jacob has come into the picture. He became the
leader and father of the children of Israel, in place of his elder
twin brother, but he could equally be called the inventor of cheating.
His blind father was misled into giving him the blessing due to the
first-born. He knew how to acquire a goodly portion of his uncle's
sheep. Nevertheless, the Divine blessing went with him. He had the
qualities of mind that his descendents would need. But he developed
in sin as he did in cleverness. So it was also with others. From hero
to hero the path of Man downwards can be followed. The fall of Man
has been an evolving process which in a sense continues up to this
day. New forms of wrong are often being invented. No sooner is one
kind familiar enough to nullify itself than another is discovered.
King David, without whose heroic career the history of the children of
Israel would have been cut short, nevertheless found it in his heart
to send one of his captains into the forefront of the battle to be killed
because he coveted his wife. Such a device would not be so success-
ful today, because the captain would be likely to become suspicious.
Not just the great ones, but ordinary people have in the course of
time been expert in learning the ways of wickedness. So it is that
in the history of man's evolving capacities there is also the dark
thread of the continuing fall into evil.

That which is shown in the composition of the Bible is found again
more and more in the results of investigations in Archaeology. It
had been expected that the deeper the archaeologists dug into the
lower levels of the past, the more evidence would be found of the
primitive beginnings of human existence. But recent discoveries have
not supported this assumption. The ancient cities of Crete, which
were many, turn out to have had a kind of civilisation in advance of
the early Greek and Roman cities which came later. Why, one is
obliged to ask, did the early Greeks who learnt so much from the
Cretans, not take their cities as their model? Why has so much, which
was earlier better and more advanced, been lost in the meantime, until
the modern image of a city was produced? The diggings in the ancient
city of Jericho brought to light evidence of ancient cities at the
lowest level of a higher grade than those above. How can one hear
that underneath the oldest of these was found at the lowest level a
sacred shrine, without being reminded that at the furthest beginning
of human history is the tradition of the garden shared by God and Man?

The furthest back that the knowledgeable mind can penetrate does not reveal the primitive beginning out of which everything else has followed, step by step, to a higher level. It reveals instead the picture of a beginning illumined by the light of Heaven and filled with its harmony out of which there followed the fall of Man into struggle and wrong.

Redemption

The third fact of evolution which is spoken of in the Bible as the history of evolution is the redemption of Man. Put in its simplest form the old prophetic words may be quoted: "God has visited his people." The serpent invaded the Garden of Paradise from outside. Christ, coming from Heaven to earth to work for the redemption of Man, came likewise from outside, invading earth existence. There was nothing in the life of Mankind to be sufficient to bring salvation in the dilemma into which the interference of evil had plunged human souls. The greatest leaders who most clearly retained a reflection of the divine image in which Man had been created could preserve themselves from evil, but not others. In all those in whom the original pattern was in part preserved, foremost was Jesus of Nazareth. The Christians of a later time, who regarded Him as being the highest and most perfect pattern of a human being, had much right on their side. Nevertheless, He came forth from the human world on earth. He, out of Himself, was not able to bring about the redemption of Man, nor even to transmit His image to the people round Him. As Rudolf Steiner made very clear in his studies on Christianity, only a Divine Being, coming from the world of God beyond the earth, could bring such cosmic power to Man that the fall into evil could be overcome. The serpent came from the world of the gods. Only one of the Sons of God could withstand and overcome it. Mankind had been caught in a struggle between gods, although his existence was lived on the earth. The battle between good and evil, although it is experienced as a human one, is in fact an affair of the gods into which Mankind has been drawn. In the third great event of human evolution the history made among the gods invaded the history of Man on earth.

The Logos, the world creating Word, descended in Christ from the heights of the Heavens to make His dwelling in the human soul and body of Jesus. The hour of this happening was that in which

John the Baptist baptised Jesus in the river Jordan. Christ in Jesus lived for a short while on earth, entered into death on the Cross and fought the cosmic fight with the power of evil and death. When the Resurrection was achieved at the first Easter, the way was opened for the redemption of Man. In the theology of past centuries an unfortunate misunderstanding has arisen. The custom came about of looking at this event as if it had happened completely, once and for all, at one moment of time. Christian people, filled with faith, would have the duty of looking back on this event, remembering it and believing in it. Another way of thinking would be more realistic. The fall of Man once released a long process of evolving into human existence. Sin and wrong had not remained the same in the course of the centuries. The event of the Resurrection likewise released new cosmic forces of life into history. That which can be called redemption is in reality an historic process which began at the first Easter and continues in our time and on into the future. Rudolf Steiner described the event on Golgotha as the turning point in human evolution. Expressed in a diagram a line could be drawn downwards from the original birth of Man out of God, from the existence in Paradise, to the lowest point where the Cross would be drawn. The process of the fall would be represented in a continuing line downwards. But from the point where the Cross stands, another line would be drawn pointing upwards towards an end point where the Holy City stands. Man's history would be seen in the design of the way down from the Garden and upwards towards the City at the end of time. God gave Man shelter in the Garden at the beginning. Man is required to build the city, where, at the fulfilment of history, God and Man will dwell together. Man was born out of God and at the end should join God because through the working of Christ, he should be able to work his way upwards into a new divinely inspired nature. Man will join God because, through Christ, he will become godlike.

The Father in Heaven

When Christ descended into Man's life on earth, He spoke of Himself as the Son of God. He spoke of God as the Father in the Heavens, giving to His hearers the picture of Himself as the Son sent out to do a work on behalf of the Father, looking back to Him as the source of His being and wisdom. He gave to mankind a place in the picture. He showed him to be the son who had ventured alone into the far country and fallen a victim to the powers of evil which he could neither comprehend nor withstand. He offered to Man, to the one who was lost, a new

42

relationship to God, giving him back his sonship. He shared with the people around Him, His own trusting relationship to the Father. When they asked Him to instruct them how to pray, He offered to them the form of address He used Himself. He said, "Say, 'Our Father who art in the Heavens.' " In that hour when this prayer was prayed for the first time, a great deed was done. Man, the fallen one, was lifted up into the community of the Son of God, who had come down to earth, with the Father, Who ruled in the Heavens. By becoming man, the Son of God made Man into God. In that first hour this was an ideal for the future. But the Lord's prayer is still with us. Every time is is prayed it is one little step further on the path of evolving that leads Man to become in reality the Son of God.

When Christ spoke of Himself to the apostles as the way to the Father, He was expressing the real meaning of redemption. It is a path of evolution open to each human soul who is able to decide to go with Christ towards the meeting with the Father. It is a way of life on which the fallen nature of Man can be overcome and transformed. Risen Man will not be the same as Man was in his unspoilt form at the beginning. There is all the difference between the innocent child, with all the heavenly characteristics of its nature, and the old person in whom experience has ripened into wisdom and his goodwill into the substance of goodness. So it is in the history of Mankind. That which grows out of the encounter with temptation and the struggle with the powers of evil is the fruit which has matured from the flowering of the virtue of innocence. Man has gone forth from God, like the prodigal son to the far country, and has lost what was given to him because he could not keep himself from being involved with the powers of evil. But he has the opportunity to come to himself in the wasteland and to decide to find his own way back to the home in the Heavens. The Father waits to find again with joy the one who has been lost, to welcome back the one who, although he was lost, has found himself.

Resurrection

A new understanding of what has happened at the Resurrection is our present need. It is the beginning of the new half of Man's evolution on earth. But Man could never complete what lies ahead if Christ did not go with him. In the parable of the prodigal son a vision stands behind the words of a third One who is also a son. The two sons described at the beginning have separated, the one to stay at home, the other to go into the far country. But there is also the One who made the sacrifice of going into the dangerous country to look for the lost brother. When it says in the parable that the lost one came to himself, a new inner power has been given to him which Christ has brought to Man. How could the lost one find the strength to make the hard way back with only the powers he could find within himself? Christ was going with him on the way, giving him the strength of His Spirit as they went. Man could not find the path towards his resurrection if Christ were not his companion all the way. It is a misunderstanding to assume that after the Resurrection the Spirit of Christ withdrew again to the Heavens. In fact, the inner meaning of the appearances of the Risen One to the disciples, as they are described in the Gospels, is that He was showing them that His Spirit had been born in the overcoming of death into the evolution of Mankind on the earth. He was assuring them that He would be with human souls in the struggle for Resurrection to the end of time. The Risen One did not come to His followers in order to leave them, but to reveal to them that He would become the guide and leader of Mankind on the hard and strenuous path into the future. The Spirit of Christ does not survey the struggles of history from the distance. He stands in the midst of them, suffering with and strengthening human souls in their struggles to make history into the path towards resurrection, in their efforts to build the Holy City out of the ideals and deeds that can be undertaken here on earth. (Rudolf Steiner "From Jesus to Christ".)

The Resurrection has given true spiritual meaning to the business of living a human life on earth. The purpose of evolution is not yet achieved. The individual person cannot believe that he has reached the ideal of his risen form in one lifetime. If he is to join in the great enterprise of going from the Garden to the City, of attaining the purpose of human history, he must return from time to time to the place where the work is in hand. Although Man belongs by birth to the Universe, the place where he can join in the fulfilling of his evolution is the earth. The Universe is filled with the activities of the cosmic beings stronger and wiser than himself. In earth existence he has the opportunity to make his own history, as he cannot do on the far side of the Gates of Birth and Death. There he can be, here he can do and create. Through the continuing presence of the Spirit of Christ, uniting with Man in the effort to fulfil his destiny, the individual soul can take his place in the struggle of history. He can see with his own insight that the fulfilment of his humanity depends on joining in the destiny of all Mankind. The enthusiasm of the soul who has seen the meaning of Christ's presence in earth existence will draw him back to earth whenever he has the strength to come, that he may do his part to create the Holy City in which Man will in real truth become the Son of God again.

In the world of today there are forms of religious outlook in which the true purpose of Man is represented as the attainment of a state of perfection. It would be true to say this of such a religion as Islam, but also of the religious drive in Communism. But it would not be true to say this of Christianity. Man in the Christian sense is an evolving being. The Holy City will not be a place of continuing perfection. It will be the starting point of new epochs of evolution. But what will then happen would be within the Universe itself and not in the far country of the earth as it is at present. Christ has accepted the fallen nature of Man. He did not turn away from the sick and the sinners when in the body of Jesus. He shared human existence. He went to meet them to share with them His strength to overcome. He rejected the powers of evil, separating Himself from the Prince of this world, but He never rejected human souls who were in the wrong. He put them on the way to overcome and to cultivate in them the strength that is born of the encounter with failure, disappointment and disgust with oneself. He made the descent into the fallen world a victory over those powers which have turned against God and wished to bewitch human souls with their false ideas. The evolving of mankind has to take place in the presence of evil and in the struggle with temptation. The foundations of the Holy City are built with the strength of the will to overcome and faith in the power of the Good.

Because Resurrection is a cosmic process which takes place in the realm of the earth, the individual destinies of people in this world are of such strong significance. Whoever sees the real meaning of the presence of Christ in the history of Mankind, will feel the urgent drive to return to the body and take part again, not once but more often, in the great enterprise which is undertaken here. He will know that reincarnation is not just an idea that can be accepted within Christianity. It is a fact that can only be explained in a Christian sense. It is something which only has meaning within the purpose that has been brought into our human existence by Christ Himself. Reincarnation has its significance and will continue in the future to be a fact of our history, because Christianity is the clue to the evolution of Man.

The dead are well-informed
they look ahead beyond our bounds,
on and on further still
they gaze and they must go.
Their pilgrimage unwinds its length
their hostelries, are planets,
the shrine they seek the sun,
where newborn to the Universe
they suffer a sun-change,
being themselves like suns dispensing light.

From spaces far beyond
returning to that splendid shrine
earthward they shall incline themselves.
What is that wondrous, dreaded place
towards which the heart resolves to go,
to find its own and on its own
to will and work for what shall be?
Who walks within the dangerous dark
but He whose dwelling was the heavenly sun?
He summons the unborn to take the path
descending to the open door.
He beckons on to urgent loves and labours.